An American Bird Conservancy Compact Guide

Paul Lehman
Ornithological Editor

The American Bird Conservancy (**ABC**) is a lean, high-output, nonprofit organization practicing conservation by bringing together partners whose expertise and resources are best suited to each task. ABC is the US partner of BirdLife International, the world bird conservation partnership.

ABC supports Partners in Flight (**PIF**), an Americas-wide coalition of organizations, agencies, private companies, and individuals implementing a science-based strategy for conserving all American bird species and their habitats. Information about PIF's strategy, called *Flight Plan*, can be obtained from ABC, the National Fish and Wildlife Foundation, or the US Fish and Wildlife Service. PIF's National Coordination is on ABC's staff, and ABC implements the Flight Plan through its Globally Important Bird Area initiative.

ABC's Policy Council is a forum composed of 70 member organizations providing scientific and policy advice to conservationists; exchanging information on emerging bird conservation issues; stimulating a network of support for conservation policies; and directly accomplishing conservation through ABC. Collaboration among council organizations has assisted in the protection of numerous species, including Swainson's hawk, San Clemente loggerhead shrike, and Atlantic Coast migratory shorebirds.

ABC members receive *Bird Conservation*, the magazine about PIF and American bird conservation, and *World Birdwatch*, the magazine about bird conservation worldwide.

ALL THE
BACKYARD
BIRDS
W E S T

BY JACK L. GRIGGS

Red-shafted Flicker

HarperPerennial
A Division of HarperCollins*Publishers*

Dedicated to V. Frances Griggs

Designed by Jack L. Griggs & Peg Alrich

Edited by Virginia Croft

Illustrations reformatted by Jack E. Griggs
from the original illustrations published in
All the Birds of North America
by the following artists:

F. P. Bennett p. 29; John Dawson pp. 41–51,
73, 75; Dale Dyer pp. 77–89; Larry McQueen pp. 63–71;
Hans Peeters pp. 19–25, 31, 33, 53–61; Doug Pratt pp. 35–39;
and Andrew Vallely p. 27.

ALL THE BACKYARD BIRDS: WEST

HarperCollins books may be purchased for educational, business,
or sales promotional use. For information please write:
Special Markets Department, HarperCollins Publishers, Inc.,
10 East 53rd Street, New York, NY 10022.

FIRST EDITION

Library of Congress Cataloging-in-Publication Data
Available upon request.
ISBN 0-06-273632-9
01 02 10 9 8 7 6 5 4 3 2

CONTENTS

HOW TO ATTRACT BIRDS
a foreword by Scott Edwards 6

IDENTIFYING BACKYARD BIRDS
How to look at a bird 14
How to read the maps 16
How the birds are organized 17
Backyard birds 18

CHECKLIST AND INDEX 90

HOW TO ATTRACT BIRDS

by
SCOTT EDWARDS

There are four fundamental attractions for birds: food, water, shelter, and a place to raise their young, all of which are easily provided in backyards.

Food is the most basic and obvious bird attraction, and more birds are attracted to black-oil sunflower seeds ("oilers" to bird-feeding veterans) than to any other seed. The black-oil sunflower seeds are smaller compared to the more familiar large striped varieties. Other attractive seeds are thistle seeds, striped sunflower seeds, split peanuts, peanuts in the shell, white proso millet, and various nuts.

It is important to note that not everything labeled "birdseed" is eaten by birds. Many birdseed mixes contain filler products, seeds that add only weight and actually detract from the mix's attractiveness. Grains like milo, oats, wheat, rice, and canary seed, as well as the ambiguous "mixed grain products," are best avoided. Table scraps are not recommended for birds either. Bread crumbs, crackers, and similar foods are just empty calories that offer very little nutrition.

When most people think of bird feeding, they think first of offering seed. However, only a

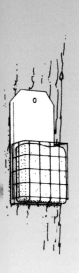

minority of the birds that surround us are seed-crushers. Many additional birds can be attracted to your feeding station if you offer suet, fruit, mealworms, or nectar.

Suet is the fat that surrounds beef kidneys. It will attract woodpeckers, chickadees, titmice, nuthatches, and brown creepers. It is also occasionally eaten by catbirds, mockingbirds, orioles, and warblers, among others. Suet is very dense and should not be confused with fat trimmings from other beef parts. Plain fat is not as beneficial, has a much higher water content, and will freeze in cold weather.

Suet is not just for winter feeding. Most commercially available suets have been rendered, meaning that they have been boiled repeatedly to remove impurities and to prevent them from going rancid. There is even "summer suet" or suet doughs that are made to survive hot weather without melting.

Suet is best attached directly to the trunk of a large deciduous tree, at least initially. This is where the birds that feed on suet look for their food in the wild.

Fruit like oranges, grapes, and bananas attract orioles and tanagers. Bug-eating birds such

7

as bluebirds, wrens, and many others readily take mealworms. And, of course, no feeding station would be complete without the presence of nectar for hummingbirds.

The accepted formula for hummingbird nectar is four to five parts water to one part plain table sugar. I don't recommend the use of commercially prepared nectars or the use of coloring. Do not use any artificial sweeteners or honey. It is important to maintain a nectar feeder regularly. Nectar ferments rapidly and can be hazardous to hummingbirds if left out for more than a day or two. Nectar should be changed more often in hot weather.

How to dispense bird food, particularly seed, is an important choice to make. There are three basic designs for seed feeders: the tube feeder, usually made of polycarbonate and designed to hang from a tree or hook; the open platform feeder, which may or may not be covered; and the hopper feeder, basically a platform feeder with a Plexiglas center (the hopper) to hold and dispense seed.

Most tube feeders are designed to dispense black-oil sunflower seeds. Nearly all of the small seed-eaters that perch on tube feeders have such a strong preference for oilers that

8

using a mixture of seeds is often counter-productive. If you are presently filling your tube feeders with mixed seeds, you probably have witnessed the birds employing a technique called "bill sweeping." By sweeping their beaks from side to side, the birds remove everything but the oilers. And you get to fill your tubes more often.

Some tube feeders have very small ports designed to dispense thistle (technically known as niger) seed. These feeders primarily attract goldfinches.

All tube feeders are designed for small birds. The jays, cardinals, grosbeaks, grackles, and woodpeckers are too big to use them. This is good for the small seed-eaters, which are often bullied off feeders that will accommodate larger birds. But if you can only have one feeder, you should consider a hopper feeder.

Hopper feeders are the most popular type, and a well-designed one will provide enough room to attract a large variety of birds. Both perching birds and ground feeders will visit a hopper feeder with a large landing area. The large seed capacity of the hopper feeder is another attractive feature for the people who have to fill them. Many hopper feeders will hold several pounds of birdseed and don't

have to be filled every day. Because of the variety of birds a hopper feeder can attract, it is an excellent place to use a high-quality mixture of seeds.

The platform or fly-through feeder attracts perhaps the widest variety of birds. The open design of these feeders allows birds to come and go from all directions. There is no dispensing mechanism to clog, so you are free to use virtually any food or combination of foods. Use peanuts in the shell if you want regular visits from jays, nutcrackers, and woodpeckers. These feeders are also ideal for serving fruit during the warmer months. I attach suet to my platform feeder to increase visits from woodpeckers, titmice, chickadees, and nuthatches.

About four times a year it is a good idea to give your feeders a thorough cleaning. Feeders can get dirty, and wet seed can mold rapidly, making a feeding station unhealthy. Once a season I take down all my feeders over the course of a few days, hose them, soak them in a strong solution of white vinegar, and scrub them with a long-handled brush designed for feeder cleaning. I use vinegar, not bleach, because of the toxicity of chlorine and the fact that it can cloud tube feeders. Regular cleaning will help ensure a healthy feeding station in your yard.

All birds must drink and bathe, so the inclusion of a birdbath with a dripper or mister will greatly enhance the attractiveness of your backyard habitat to birds, as can a recirculating pond. Drippers and misters are accessories that attach to your outside water source and provide fresh, moving water for birds. Most drippers utilize a low-flow system that constantly drips water into your water feature.

Misters spray the area around your water feature with a fine mist. They are especially effective if your water feature is surrounded by foliage. While some birds hesitate to immerse themselves, they may "leaf-bathe," an action that has them rubbing their feathers against wet leaves. Misters are also very attractive to hummingbirds, which love to fly around in the mist these accessories create.

Nest boxes are used by many birds that nest in cavities (tree hollows). Bluebirds, nuthatches, wrens, and woodpeckers are a few of the species that will accept your hospitality if you erect the appropriate nest box. Some lucky people are even able to attract screech-owls!

Nest boxes should be made of untreated, unpainted wood. Red cedar or white pine 3/4 to 1 inch thick is preferable. Preservative, paints, or stains are unnecessary and may actually be harmful. The exact dimensions of the box vary depending on which bird you are attempting to attract. This information is readily available at any good library or nature center. Nest boxes must be maintained regularly and cleaned of nesting debris after each brood fledges. Keep a logbook on the progress of the birds using your nest boxes, especially one with bluebirds in it. All nest inspections should stop approximately ten days after the eggs hatch, or the nestlings may fledge prematurely.

Habitat enhancement is really the key to attracting the most interesting birds to your backyard. Successfully attracting a wide variety and number of birds to your backyard entails more than just supplying feeders, seed, a pond, or nest boxes, however. I have dozens of different feeders at my station, but there is more bird activity per square foot in my two brush piles (conglomerations of limbs, branches, and old Christmas trees) than anywhere else in my yard.

Juncos, towhees, and native sparrows such as the white-crowned nest and feed in the brush piles, and all the little songbirds seek cover there when a Cooper's or sharp-shinned hawk comes looking for an easy meal. If a brush pile is impractical, consider letting a small section of

your backyard go wild. Don't mow, don't prune, just let it grow and watch the birds show up!

Add fruit-bearing trees to your backyard habitat (mountain ash, hackberry, mulberry, and sassafras, for example) and you can attract waxwings, mockingbirds, warblers, and bluebirds. Coniferous trees and shrubs such as juniper and holly are wonderful bird attractions and provide cover as well as food.

You can find assistance in improving the attractiveness of your backyard habitat at your local nature center and at some of the better wild bird supply stores. Don't be discouraged if your first improvements don't get immediate results. Over time your backyard can become an oasis for birds.

Keep a good pair of binoculars on your windowsill next to this guide to identify the rarer birds your feeder attracts. Binoculars for birding should be 7 or 8 power, bright, sharp, and easy to hold. Stay away from cute gadgets like zooms, perma- or insta-focus, and strange-colored lenses. If you wear eyeglasses, you should be able to leave them on while using your binoculars. The wider your binoculars' field of vision (a salesperson can explain how this is measured), the easier they will be to use.

HOW TO LOOK AT A BIRD

The way birds feed and their adaptations for feeding are the most important points to recognize in identifying and understanding a bird. For the beginner, the color and pattern of an unknown bird can be so striking that important points of shape and behavior go unnoticed. But feeding adaptations, especially bill shape, best reveal a bird's role in nature — its truest identity.

Owls, hawks, doves, woodpeckers, and many other birds are easily recognized by shape and behavior. Songbirds are more confusing. If you don't immediately recognize a songbird as a sparrow, a wren, or a warbler, for example, look at its bill shape. Is it a seed-crusher or a bug-eater? Seed-crushers have strong, conical bills for cracking seeds. The shape of a bug-eater's bill varies with the way it catches bugs.

conical bill

Most bug-eaters have slender, straight bills used to probe in trees, brush, ground litter, and rock crevices. A few have curved bills for specialized probing. And some, the flycatcher group, have broad-based, flat bills. Flycatchers catch bugs in midair, and their broad bills improve their chances of success.

straight bill

curved bill

If bill shape can't be seen, a bird's feeding behavior is often just as revealing. Sparrows

flycatching bill

14

don't flit among the branches of a tree searching for bugs, and warblers won't be seen on the ground picking at seeds.

Knowing its bill shape or feeding behavior reduces the possible identities of an unknown bird. Plumage marks can then be used to identify all the backyard species.

Most names used to describe parts of a bird are predictable — back, crown, throat, etc. Three names that might not be immediately understood are rump, undertail coverts, and wing bars. The rump is at the base of the tail, topside; undertail coverts cover the base of the tail, bottomside. Wing bars are formed by the contrasting tips (often white) of the feathers that help cover the wing when it is folded.

Underside of tail showing tail spots and undertail coverts.

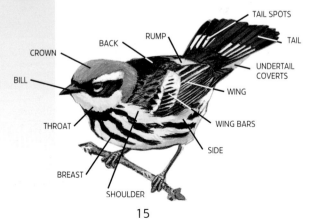

TAIL SPOTS

RUMP

BACK

TAIL

CROWN

UNDERTAIL COVERTS

BILL

WING

THROAT

WING BARS

SIDE

BREAST

SHOULDER

15

HOW TO READ THE MAPS

Range maps provide a simplified picture of a species' distribution. They indicate the birds that can be expected in any local region. Birds are not evenly distributed over their ranges. They require suitable habitat (no seeds, no sparrows) and are typically scarcest at their range limits. Some birds are numerous but not commonly seen because they are secretive.

Weather and food availability affect bird distribution in winter. Some birds regularly retreat south to escape winter weather. Others leave their northern ranges only occasionally. Some whose resident population slowly creeps northward in mild winters may perish if their newly occupied range is hit by a hard winter.

MAP KEY

SUMMER OR NESTING

WINTER

ALL YEAR

MIGRATION
(spring & fall)

HOW THE BIRDS ARE ORGANIZED

NOCTURNAL
nighthawk, owls   18

AERIALISTS
vulture, condor, hawks, swallows, hummingbirds   20

GROUND-WALKERS
quails, pheasant, doves, pigeon   30

TREE-CLIMBERS
woodpeckers, flicker, nuthatches, creeper   34

FLYCATCHING BILLS
flycatcher, kingbirds, waxwing, phoebes   40

CURVED BILLS
thrasher, wrens   44

STRAIGHT BILLS
BLUEBIRD-SIZE AND LARGER   46
*mockingbird, magpie, raven, crows,
jays, starling, cowbird, blackbirds, oriole,
meadowlark, tanager, robin, catbird, bluebirds*

WARBLER-SIZE AND SMALLER   62
*warblers, titmice, chickadees,
bushtit, kinglets*

CONICAL BILLS   72
*towhees, grosbeaks, finches, siskin,
junco, sparrows*

OWLS AND NIGHTHAWK

GREAT HORNED OWL

BARN OWL

COMMON NIGHTHAWK

The western screech-owl has yellow eyes and distinctive horns but is only about the size of a man's hand. It visits woodsy parks and neighborhoods.

Because they hunt in the evenings and at night, owls are not often seen in backyards — or anywhere else. But some of the more common owls live close to civilization and are likely to be heard. The great horned owl has proved particularly adaptable. It is the 800-pound gorilla of the bird world and goes almost anywhere it wants to, including parks and suburbs. It is large enough to take rabbits and ducks.

The **great horned owl** gives a series of distinctive low hoots in various rhythms: *hoo, hoo-hoo, hoo, hoo* or *hoo-hoo-hoo, hoo-hoo, hoo*, for instance. It is a massive bird with yellow eyes and large ear tufts, or "horns," which are usually raised and obvious.

Barn owls don't hoot but give a screech or rasping hiss. The white heart-shaped face set with dark eyes is its best visual mark. Barn owls hunt over fields and agricultural land. They fly close to the ground and are too often seen as road kill as a result of collisions with cars.

Nighthawks sweep through the sky feeding like swifts or swallows. They are common over open country and some towns and cities at dusk and dawn — sometimes in daylight. Note the **nighthawk's** white wing patch and listen for its nasal *peent* flight call.

18

Common
Nighthawk

Great Horned
Owl

Barn Owl

VULTURE AND CONDOR

TURKEY VULTURE

Large black birds with unfeathered heads tugging at a piece of road kill are easily recognized as vultures – the "buzzards" of the old West. And since there is only one vulture throughout most of the West, the **turkey vulture,** identification is not a problem. Adults are the ones with red heads. Young turkey vultures are dark-headed.

When not feeding, vultures are usually seen soaring high overhead in search of carrion. Even at a great distance, they can often be recognized by their flight style and the contrasting pattern of pale and dark on their underwing. Turkey vultures often tip a bit from side to side as they soar and usually hold their wings above horizontal in a shallow V.

In southwestern deserts, the zone-tailed hawk mimics the flight and appearance of the turkey vulture in order to closely approach ground prey. White tail bands and a feathered head are its best distinguishing marks.

Certainly not a common bird, the California condor is being nurtured back from near extinction. It has been reintroduced in Los Padres National Forest of California, and recently young birds have been released at the Grand Canyon, where they are more likely to be seen.

Young **California condors** (releases are all young birds) have dark heads. Their greater size and underwing pattern distinguish condors from vultures even at a distance.

20

young

Turkey Vulture

California Condor

HAWKS

KESTREL

RED-TAILED HAWK

The white-tailed kite is a hawk of open lands that has adapted to grassy highway borders in California, where it scans for rodents from a perch or hover.

The white-tailed kite is pale gray above with black shoulders, and white below with black wrist patches.

The kestrel and red-tailed hawk are not likely to be seen in backyards, but they are common along roads and in parks. A kestrel hunts from a perch, typically a wire or pole overlooking a vacant lot or other open area. It will often return to the same perch daily if it is successful in capturing the mice, large insects, or small birds that are its prey. Kestrels often hover over suspected prey.

The **kestrel** is identified by its small size, only 10 to 12 inches long, and two black face streaks contrasting with its white cheeks and throat. Males are smaller than females, and the blue on the male's wings contrasts sharply with the red on its back and tail. The female is an even red above, with heavy dark barring.

Red-tailed hawks are likely to be seen soaring overhead or perched on a roadside pole. Plumage varies considerably, but nearly all adults have a distinctive red tail (pink from below), with or without narrow dark tail bands. Young birds have brownish tails with many narrow dark bands. The dark streaking that often forms a band across a red-tail's belly is a good mark for many birds. And the dark bar along the leading edge of the underwing is a sure mark for identifying soaring birds.

pale form

Kestrel

♀

♂

♂

intermediate form

dark form

Red-tailed Hawk

pale form

intermediate form

young

young

HAWKS

COOPER'S HAWK

SHARP-SHINNED HAWK

Young hawks of some larger species (buteos) can be confused with a young Cooper's, but they don't attack at backyard feeders as a Cooper's does. And a Cooper's seldom sits openly on roadside perches, as buteos do.

Cooper's and sharp-shinned hawks are the birds of prey known for attacking songbirds at backyard bird feeders and sometimes colliding with picture windows. They seldom perch openly like the hawks described on the previous page. Instead, they typically lurk in foliage until prey appears and then, with a sprinter's explosive burst, ambush the unsuspecting dinner.

Except in size, the two species are nearly identical. Both **Cooper's** and the **sharp-shinned** have long tails with distinctive broad dark and pale bands. Adults are blue-gray above with rusty barring below. Young birds are brown above and have brown streaking on their underparts.

Size differences between Cooper's and the sharp-shinned can be hard to judge. A small male sharpie (about 12 inches long) can be distinguished from a large female Cooper's (about 18 inches), but most individuals are somewhere in between. Small differences in their tails are the best marks separating the two species but are very difficult to see. The tip of a Cooper's tail is round and banded white. The sharpie's tail has squarer corners and a narrow gray terminal band.

24

Typical variations in
sharp-shinned hawk's tail

sharp-shinned
young

Cooper's

young

Cooper's young

sharp-shinned

young

adults shown in typical
flight; young birds soaring

Cooper's Hawk

young

**Sharp-shinned
Hawk**

young

SWALLOWS

CLIFF SWALLOW

TREE SWALLOW

BARN SWALLOW

Two other species are brown above and white below like young tree swallows. The bank swallow has a brown breast band; the rough-winged, a dirty-brown throat and upper breast.

Swallows are sleek and speedy aerialists that spend most of their day capturing bugs in flight. Because flying insects abound near water, swallows often fly over water. When not feeding, they can often be seen together, side by side on a wire by the dozens. Tree swallows commonly nest in boxes. Barn and cliff swallows make mud nests, often under eaves and bridges. The barn swallow's nest is cup shaped; the cliff swallow's, gourd shaped.

It isn't easy to get a good look at a flying swallow, but most species can be identified at a glance if you know what to look for. The **tree swallow** is white below and glossy blue-green above. (White on the similar violet-green swallow extends high onto the rump.) Young birds are brown above. Note that the tree swallow doesn't have a "swallowtail."

The **barn swallow** is the swallow with the tail shape that has become a graphic symbol of speed and grace. The upperparts are a deep blue on all birds, but the orange-buff under-parts can be paler on young birds. Young birds can also have shorter tail streamers.

The **cliff swallow** has a nearly square tail. Its buff rump contrasts with the dark back, and its dark throat contrasts with the pale breast and belly.

26

young

young

Cliff Swallow

Tree Swallow

Barn Swallow

HUMMING-BIRDS

RUFOUS HUMMINGBIRD

ANNA'S HUMMINGBIRD

BLACK-CHINNED HUMMINGBIRD

BROAD-TAILED HUMMINGBIRD

The jewel-like reflections from the throats (gorgets) of male hummers are only visible at favorable angles; most often the gorget appears dark. Watch for a flash of the gorget color as a hummer turns its head. Female hummers lack the male's distinctive gorget and can be very difficult to separate.

The rusty-colored back and sides of the male **rufous hummingbird** are an easy mark. Females have green backs. Along the coast of California, Allen's hummingbird is similar, but the adult male has a green back.

Anna's hummingbird is the most common hummer in West Coast backyards. The male has a rose-red crown and a flared gorget. The female is a bulky-looking version of the female black-chinned, with dingier-colored sides. Anna's is a bit larger than most hummers.

It is the band of purple on the male **black-chinned hummingbird's** gorget that is the important mark. Females are whitish below with a buff tinge on the sides.

Throughout much of the Rocky Mountains, the **broad-tailed hummingbird** is a regular at feeders. The male has a rose-red gorget; females look like female rufous hummers but are larger, with fuller tails and paler sides.

Rufous Hummingbird

♂

♀ rufous

Anna's Hummingbird

♂

♀ black chinned

♂

Black-chinned Hummingbird

♂

Broad-tailed Hummingbird

GAMEBIRDS

CALIFORNIA QUAIL

GAMBEL'S QUAIL

RING-NECKED PHEASANT

California quail can be separated from Gambel's by their call. The California gives a loud *chi-ca-go;* Gambel's adds a syllable, *chi-ca-go-go.*

Gamebirds have learned to be very cautious and to stay hidden for good reason. They are prey to many wild animals, as well as humans. Only a few gamebirds are found on cultivated land or in areas near people.

Quail venture into rural towns and backyards. They live and forage together in coveys (small flocks) most of the time. When nesting and raising young, they are paired. At night, they roost in trees for safety. The California quail is widespread; Gambel's is associated with desert scrub.

These are the only quail with teardrop-shaped plumes on their heads. The best marks separating them are on their bellies. The **California quail** has a scaled belly. The belly of **Gambel's quail** varies with sex. Males have a large black spot on their buff bellies that is lacking in females.

Ring-necked pheasants were introduced from Asia and are one of the few introduced gamebirds to become established. Some males have green bodies; others have white wings; some lack the neck ring. All males have a red eye patch. The most common form is illustrated. Both sexes have distinctive long pointed tails.

30

California Quail

Gambel's Quail

Ring-necked Pheasant

DOVES

BAND-TAILED PIGEON

MOURNING DOVE

ROCK DOVE

A flock of band-tailed pigeons flying in the distance can be distinguished from rock doves by their uniformity; rock dove plumages vary.

D oves (or pigeons — there is no difference) can be depended on to show up at backyard feeders. They have very short legs and walk on the ground like gamebirds rather than hopping along like most birds. As they walk, they bob their heads back and forth in a characteristic fashion.

In the wild, where they are declining in some regions, band-tailed pigeons take mostly seeds and acorns. Some venture into parks and backyards for seeds or the berries of ornamental plants. The white bar on the back of the neck and the namesake band of gray on the tip of the **band-tailed pigeon's** tail are sure marks separating it from dark variations of the rock dove.

Mourning doves and rock doves are widespread and abundant. **Mourning doves** are the ones with long pointed tails. A mournful call, *woo-oó-oo, oo, oo, oo,* is given in spring and summer by unmated males.

Rock dove is the formal name for the well-known pigeon of cities and farms. Pigeons have colonized most of the world in the company of man. The many color variations seen are the result of interbreeding with exotic domesticated strains. The ancestral form is shown in the foreground.

32

Band-tailed Pigeon

Mourning Dove

Rock Dove

WOOD-PECKERS

DOWNY WOODPECKER

HAIRY WOODPECKER

The pileated woodpecker is sometimes seen in mature trees in parks or woodlots. It is a large, mostly black bird the size of a crow, with a pointed, flaming red crest and white patches in its wings.

The most common backyard woodpecker is the downy. It is also the smallest, just 7 inches long. The hairy woodpecker has virtually the identical plumage pattern but is 2 inches larger. Some forms of both species may have very few wing spots and/or a brownish gray cast to their white plumage.

The size difference is easy to recognize when the two species are seen side by side, but can be hard to judge when the birds are seen separately. The best mark is the bill length. The **hairy woodpecker** has a much larger bill — nearly as long as its head. The **downy woodpecker's** bill extends only about half its head length.

Males of both species have a bright red patch on the back of their crowns that is lacking in females. Young birds of both sexes also show a patch of red on their heads, but the color is more diffuse and is located on the center or forepart of the crown rather than on the rear.

There is a very small plumage difference that can be noted at close range on most birds. The hairy's white outer tail feathers are unmarked, while the downy's are marked with two or more black bars.

young

hairy

Downy
Woodpecker

♀

♂

♀

Hairy
Woodpecker

♂

WOOD-PECKERS

LADDER-BACKED WOODPECKER

RED-SHAFTED FLICKER

ACORN WOODPECKER

Nuttall's woodpecker replaces the ladder-backed in parts of California. The only notable differences are in the black and white face pattern.

The woodpeckers shown on these pages seldom show up at suet or seed feeders. The red-shafted flicker is usually seen on the ground in open short-grass areas such as lawns or parks, where it feeds on ants, its favorite meal. Like other woodpeckers, flickers gather insects from trees, but because they often feed on the ground, they are sometimes not recognized as woodpeckers.

The typical view of a **red-shafted flicker** is of a white-rumped bird rising in flight from the ground and flying directly away, flashing red in the underwing. Seen closer, the flicker has strikingly patterned plumage. The male has a red mustache mark lacking in females.

Ladder-backed woodpeckers are common in residential areas of the desert Southwest. They nest and feed in cactus as well as trees. The **ladder-backed woodpecker** is the same size as the similar downy woodpecker on the previous page, but has horizontal bars on its back instead of a white vertical stripe.

Acorn woodpeckers are common in parks and suburbs, usually in small noisy groups. They drill holes in trees (sometimes in buildings) for storage of acorns. **Acorn woodpeckers** are unmistakable. The red on the crown of the female is more restricted than in the male.

Ladder-backed Woodpecker

♀

♂

Red-shafted Flicker

♂

Acorn Woodpecker

♀

♂

NUTHATCHES AND CREEPER

WHITE-BREASTED NUTHATCH

RED-BREASTED NUTHATCH

BROWN CREEPER

The pygmy nuthatch is found in pine forest. It is just a bit smaller than the red-breasted and is distinguished by its gray-brown cap and pale spot on its hind neck.

Not all birds seen climbing a tree trunk are woodpeckers. Nuthatches and the brown creeper also make a living on the insects and larvae hidden in a tree's bark. Nuthatches are the only tree-climbers so agile that they can creep *down* a tree. Presumably they find morsels that upward-climbers miss. They also forage for insects at the tips of small branches and take seeds from pine cones.

The **white-breasted nuthatch** is the most common nuthatch at most feeders. It is dark above and white below with an inconspicuous wash of rusty red on its flanks. Females are the same as males, except some are notice-ably grayer on the crown.

Red-breasted nuthatches prefer conifers. They are smaller than the white-breasted, have a rusty-red breast and belly, and sport a white stripe above the eye. Females are noticeably duller than males.

The **brown creeper** is often overlooked. It can appear on the trunk of any tree, especially mature ones, and blends into the background of bark. It spirals up a tree trunk searching for insects and is often not noticed until it flies from one tree to the base of another.

White-breasted Nuthatch

♀

Red-breasted Nuthatch

♂

Brown Creeper

FLYCATCHER AND KINGBIRDS

ASH-THROATED
FLYCATCHER

WESTERN
KINGBIRD

EASTERN
KINGBIRD

Cassin's kingbird can also be recognized by its call, a rough, nasal *che-bew.* Western kingbirds give a single sharp note, *kip!*

Eastern and western kingbirds are fly-catchers like the ash-throated flycatcher shown here and the phoebes on the following pages. All wait patiently on an open perch for an insect to pass by. After catching the bug midair, the flycatcher often returns to the same perch to repeat the process. Flycatchers are tolerant of people and tend to gather wherever flying insects are available.

Kingbirds are particularly conspicuous because of their noisy, aggressive behavior. The white-tipped tail is the sure mark for the **eastern kingbird,** which actually ranges a bit farther west in Canada than the western kingbird.

Western kingbirds and **ash-throated fly-catchers** look similar but have differences. Note the pale throat and upper breast of the western kingbird and the white edges to its black tail. The ash-throated flycatcher flashes a rusty red in its wings and tail when it flies.

The western kingbird has an even closer look-alike, Cassin's kingbird, which lives in the high, open lands of Arizona, New Mexico, Utah, Wyoming, and Colorado. There is also a pop-ulation in California's coastal foothills. Cassin's is darker gray than the western, making the white throat appear more prominent. Its tail lacks white edges and has a dusky tip.

40

Ash-throated Flycatcher

Western Kingbird

Eastern Kingbird

WAXWING AND PHOEBES

CEDAR WAXWING

SAY'S PHOEBE

BLACK PHOEBE

Vermilion flycatchers are common in parts of the Southwest. The male is vermilion and black; the female a bit like Say's phoebe but has a white throat and streaked breast.

Waxwings wander in flocks of up to a hundred birds or so except when nesting. They keep in close contact, giving a pleasing high-pitched, lisping call. A flock of these sleek birds will often sit awhile in the top of a tall tree before flying down to feed on fruit or berries. They also catch insects, flycatcher fashion, in summer.

The tiny dots of red on its wings are the source of the waxwing's name. They suggest the wax once used for sealing documents. The crest, narrow dark mask, and yellow tail tip are the easiest marks for identifying the **cedar waxwing**.

Both the black phoebe and Say's phoebe are common and tame around buildings. The black phoebe is especially attracted to water. It often flycatches from a low perch, capturing bugs close to the ground. The black upper-parts and white belly of the **black phoebe** might suggest a junco (p. 80) at first glance, but the two birds don't feed or behave at all like each other.

Say's phoebe prefers arid habitats in summer, where it sometimes flycatches from a boulder when a fence or bush is not available. The combination of tawny underparts and unstreaked gray throat is distinctive for **Say's phoebe.**

42

Cedar Waxwing

young

Say's Phoebe

Black Phoebe

CALIFORNIA THRASHER

HOUSE WREN

BEWICK'S WREN

The most common thrasher of the Southwest is the curve-billed thrasher. It has blurry breast spots.

A few birds have curved bills that they use to probe for bugs. Thrashers use their bills to rake the soil and leaf litter under shrubs and bushes for insects. Because they are shy and often hidden, thrashers are frequently heard picking through the debris under a bush before they are seen. When surprised, they run or fly low and swiftly into a nearby bush.

The most common thrasher is the **California thrasher.** It is chocolate brown above, russet under the tail, and has a faint white eyebrow. Other thrashers (several species occur in the Southwest) are grayer backed and lack the eyebrow; some have breast spots.

Wrens are not likely to be confused with other birds, even if their slightly curved bill is not noticed. No other small gray-brown bird has similar fine barring on its wings and tail, and none cock their tail or scold so expressively.

Both Bewick's and house wrens are familiar in brushy residential neighborhoods; Bewick's is a bit larger. **House wrens** have a faint eye-brow at best, whereas **Bewick's wren** has a prominent white eyebrow. Bewick's also has white corners in its tail and is whiter below than the house wren. The grayer form of Bewick's is the one seen in the West.

California Thrasher

House Wren

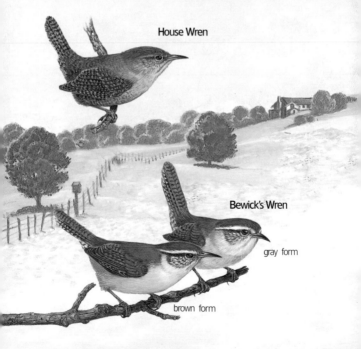

Bewick's Wren

gray form

brown form

MOCKINGBIRD AND MAGPIE

MOCKINGBIRD

BLACK-BILLED MAGPIE

One bird, the logger-head shrike, resembles the mockingbird. It is not seen in back-yards but can be found sometimes on roadside fences or wires in open country.

The loggerhead shrike has a shorter bill, a black mask, and a different pattern of white in its wings.

One of the most common and familiar birds in its range, the mockingbird will perch conspicuously on wires, limbs, or often a TV antenna and serenade tirelessly throughout the year, even into the night. It is a famous mimic and will repeat grating, mechanical sounds as readily as the songs of other birds. When perched, the **mockingbird** is a slim gray bird with mostly dark wings and a long, dark tail that it often holds erect. When it takes flight, the white in the wings becomes a prominent mark.

Magpies usually occur in small noisy flocks and are common in rural communities and over farm and range land, especially along streams. They are closely related to jays and crows and, like them, feed on whatever is available, including seeds, insects, and small rodents. Magpies make large, conspicuous, domed nests in trees or shrubs.

The **black-billed magpie's** streaming, dark green, iridescent tail is as strikingly obvious as its black-and-white plumage pattern. Its high, whining *mahg?* call is also distinctive. West of the Sierra Nevada in California, magpies have yellow bills and yellow eye patches and are considered a different species, the yellow-billed magpie.

46

young

Mockingbird

loggerhead
shrike

mockingbird

Black-billed Magpie

RAVENS AND CROWS

The great-tailed grackle is increasingly common in the Southwest. Males are large all-black birds with very large tails.

Crows and their larger relatives, ravens, are the most intelligent North American birds. It is an opinion rooted in Native American folklore and confirmed by present-day ornithologists. Crows and ravens are not restricted to a specific diet but will take whatever is available. Their adaptability has permitted them to flourish. Crows are found everywhere except in deserts, mountain forests, and the Arctic. And ravens manage to live year-round even in northernmost Alaska.

Scientists recognize two crow species in the West, the American crow and the northwestern crow. The two species are virtually indistin-guishable in the field. Those crows found on the Pacific coast from Puget Sound to Alaska are considered to be northwestern crows.

Separating the much larger **common raven** from the **American crow** is usually just a matter of estimating size and noting tail shape. However, there is the Chihuahuan raven that is about the size of a large crow or a small raven and can be confused with either. It is often found in large flocks at farms and dumps in winter, but only in the Southwest north to southeast Colorado and east to central Texas. Crows give a distinctive *caw* or *cah*. Ravens have a hoarse, low-pitched *c-r-ock* call, higher in the Chihuahuan raven.

48

American Crow

Common Raven

PINYON JAY

WESTERN SCRUB-JAY

STELLER'S JAY

If you are camping in northern conifers, chances are your "backyard" bird is a gray jay (gray, crest-less, small bill). These fearless "camp-robbers" boldy steal from tent and table.

Scrub-jays and Steller's jays boldly come to backyard feeders for seeds in all seasons. Pinyon jays are much rarer, primarily winter, visitors to neighborhoods and backyard feeders.

Most jays, including Steller's and scrub-jays, are slim birds with long tails. However, the pinyon jay is shaped like a small crow. It behaves and flies like one as well and is often found in large flocks. The sky-blue plumage of the **pinyon jay** is darkest on the head. The throat is gray with fine blue streaks.

The bird widely known as a scrub jay is now believed to be several species. The wide-spread western species has been named the western scrub-jay. The intensity of the **western scrub-jay's** blues and grays varies regionally, but the pattern remains the same. Scrub-jays store acorns for winter and are well known for taking bright trinkets and adding them to their cache.

The prominent crest and black foreparts are easy marks for identifying **Steller's jay.** The streaks on the eyebrow, chin, and crest vary regionally. They can be blue or white or may even be absent. Steller's jay is also likely to be seen in the conifers of a park or woodlot, where it feeds primarily on nuts and seeds.

50

young

Pinyon Jay

Western
Scrub-jay

Steller's Jay

young

PARK

STARLING AND COWBIRD

STARLING

BROWN-HEADED COWBIRD

The bronzed cowbird is found in parts of the Southwest. It has red eyes and a noticeably larger bill than the brown-headed.

Both starlings and cowbirds are a serious threat to other western species. Originally introduced from Europe to the New York area, the starling rapidly spread across the United States and southern Canada. It nests in cavities and has displaced native cavity-nesters such as the western bluebird (p. 60), purple martin, and Lewis' woodpecker.

The **starling's** plumage varies by season from spotted to glossy black. The birds have short tails and long pointed bills. The **brown-headed cowbird's** best mark is its conical bill. (The bird is illustrated here rather than with other conically billed birds because it most resembles a blackbird.) Males are black with a dark brown head; females, a dull gray-brown.

Cowbirds were originally birds of the Great Plains and were then known as "buffalo birds." They spread across the continent as man converted forest to farmland. Cowbirds are nest parasites. They lay an egg in other birds' nests, and the host birds raise the cowbird chick, usually at the expense of their own young. The cowbird's threat to some species is so serious that many bird conservationists give the problem top priority. However, the bird did not create the problem. We created it by altering the landscape.

young

fall

Starling

spring

molting young ♂ in fall

Brown-headed Cowbird

♀

♂

BLACKBIRDS

YELLOW-HEADED BLACKBIRD

BREWER'S BLACKBIRD

RED-WINGED BLACKBIRD

Male great-tailed grackles might be confused with Brewer's blackbird. See the sidebar on p. 48.

All the blackbirds live in flocks. In winter, they are frequently seen in mixed flocks that can include cowbirds and starlings. Only red-winged and Brewer's blackbirds are common at feeding stations.

Yellow-headed blackbirds nest in freshwater marshlands and feed in nearby fields and farmlands. Male and female **yellow-headed blackbirds** are strikingly different, with the female being smaller, browner, and showing yellow only on her throat and breast.

Preferring fields to marshes, Brewer's blackbird has spread across much of the continent as ranching and dairy farming have created its preferred habitat. It is now the most commonly seen blackbird in the West and can be found in parking lots as well as backyards. Male **Brewer's blackbirds** have yellow eyes and a metallic sheen that shows in good light. Females are gray-brown with dark eyes.

It is the male **red-winged blackbird** that is usually seen in backyards; females are shier. Females look like big streaked sparrows but have a blackbird's bill. The male's orange-red shoulders are often hidden with only the buff edges showing. The buff is absent in birds of California's Central Valley.

Yellow-headed Blackbird

♂

♀

♂

♀

Brewer's Blackbird

Red-winged Blackbird

♂

♀

ORIOLE AND MEADOWLARK

BULLOCK'S ORIOLE

WESTERN MEADOWLARK

Hooded orioles come to nectar feeders, especially in the Southwest, and Scott's oriole might be seen in ornamental growth.

The male Scott's is black and yellow, including a black hood. The male hooded is yellow to orange with black markings, including a distinctive solid black tail — but no hood.

Although more brightly colored than blackbirds, meadowlarks and orioles belong to the same family as blackbirds. The most telling similarity is bill shape.

Orioles visit parks, orchards, and residential shade trees. They sometimes visit backyard feeding stations for orange halves or a sugar-water feeder like that set out for hummingbirds. The nest of a Bullock's oriole is a conspicuous, large oval bag, often attached to the twigs on the outer branch of a large shade tree.

Male and female **Bullock's orioles** have different plumages. The adult male is bright and distinctive; note especially the large white wing patch. Females and yearling males lack the wing patch and the warm orange tones on the face and body. They are yellow on the face, breast, and under the tail, blending to pale gray on the belly. The yearling male has a black throat and eyeline.

The **western meadowlark** is well known for its black V on a bright yellow breast. It is a common roadside bird, often perching on posts or wires to deliver its rich, flute-like song. The white in the tail is also a good mark as it flies away on stiff wings with shallow strokes and short glides.

young ♂

Bullock's Oriole

♀

♂

Western Meadowlark

winter

summer

TANAGER AND ROBIN

WESTERN TANAGER

ROBIN

Summer tanagers of the Southwest are shaped like western tanagers, but males are bright red overall. Females lack the western tanager's wing bars.

The varied thrush is a relative of the robin found in moist coniferous forests. Males are orange below and have black breast bands.

➤

Western tanagers are not common in residential areas, but they are regular spring migrants and summer visitors in shade trees. More are not seen because they are relatively slow-moving birds that often stay hidden in the canopy of mature trees.

The male **western tanager** is spectacular in his brilliant summer plumage, but by fall he begins to molt to a female-like yellow-green dress. His wings and tail remain black, however, distinguishing him from the female.

The plumage of the female western tanager is much like that of the female oriole, greenish yellow below and olive gray above with two wing bars. Shape, especially bill shape, is the best mark separating the two. The tanager is more compact; its bill is shorter and more swollen than the long pointed bill of the oriole.

One of the first birds a child learns to recognize is the robin. But how many people ever notice that female **robins** are distinctively paler gray above and paler orange below than males? Young birds are heavily spotted.

The songs of both birds are somewhat similar: whistled flute-like notes given in short phrases. The tanager's song has a burrier tone.

spring ♂

♀

Western Tanager

Robin

young

CATBIRD AND BLUEBIRDS

CATBIRD

MOUNTAIN BLUEBIRD

WESTERN BLUEBIRD

The lazuli bunting often visits weedy fields. It suggests a western bluebird at first glance, but note the seed-crusher bill and the wing bars.

The catbird is a skulker, much more common in the bushes and thickets of backyards and parks than many bird watchers suspect. Its name comes from a cat-like mewing that it often makes. The only distinctive marks on the plain gray **catbird** are the rusty patch under the base of the tail, which is hard to see, and the black cap.

Both mountain and western bluebirds use boxes for nesting, as well as hollows in trees. There is much competition for nest sites with starlings (p. 52), house sparrows (p. 84), and tree swallows (p. 26).

Mountain bluebirds range from foothills to the treeline. They flycatch but more often perch or hover over open ground and flutter down to capture ground insects. Blue in the female **mountain bluebird** is limited to the rump, tail, and wings. Males are truly blue.

The female **western bluebird** is paler than the impressive male, with bright blue only in the wings and tail. The blue is palest in young birds, which also have spotting on their backs and breasts. Family groups are often seen together throughout the summer in parks and suburbs. Western bluebirds capture bugs on the ground, much as mountain bluebirds do.

Catbird

♀

♂

Mountain
Bluebird

♀

Western
Bluebird

♂

WARBLERS

TOWNSEND'S
WARBLER

AUDUBON'S
WARBLER

Audubon's warbler
and the myrtle war-
bler are now consid-
ered the same species
by ornithologists, who
call it the yellow-
rumped warbler.

The myrtle warbler
nests in the North
and occurs in small
numbers in the West
in winter and
migration. Its most
obvious difference
from Audubon's is its
white throat.

Eighteen different kinds of warblers —
each more beautiful than the other —
nest in or migrate through western North
America. Almost any of them might conceiv-
ably choose your backyard for a brief layover.
Audubon's warbler is one of the most likely
visitors; Townsend's warbler is more likely to
be seen at a park, especially in conifers.

To identify any warbler, begin by noting
whether or not it shows yellow and whether
or not it has wing bars. If you get these
two marks first and then note other prominent features, you will have the best chance
of success.

Audubon's and Townsend's warblers show
yellow and have wing bars. **Townsend's
warbler** has yellow concentrated on the face
and breast. Spring males have a black crown,
eye patch, and bib. These markings are duller
in females and young birds, both of which
lack the bib.

All plumages of **Audubon's warbler** have
a yellow rump. There are also distinctive
patches of yellow on the throat and on the
side near the shoulder, although sometimes
faint on young birds in fall. Spring males have
a yellow crown. Audubon's warbler is widespread and abundant, even in winter.

62

spring ♂

♀

Townsend's Warbler

Audubon's Warbler

young

spring ♂

spring ♀

WARBLERS

ORANGE-CROWNED WARBLER

YELLOW WARBLER

Yellow and orange-crowned warblers may also be separated by their song and call notes.

The yellow warbler has a sweet song and a rich *chip* call. The orange-crowned's song is a thin trill; its call, a metallic *chip*.

Two of the most common and widespread warblers in the West are the orange-crowned and the yellow warblers. Both frequent bushes, shrubs, and the lower limbs of trees and are conspicuous. They are likely to be seen in residential neighborhoods, especially if there is water nearby.

Orange-crowned and yellow warblers show yellow but have no wing bars. At their plumage extremes, the two species should not be confused. The **yellow warbler** is virtually all yellow. Males are bright and have chestnut breast streaks. The identification problem occurs among some of the duller fall females.

As in many warblers, the plumage of the yellow warbler varies with sex, age, and season. A young yellow warbler in fall can be greenish and duller than some orange-crowned warblers. On dull yellow warblers, look for the beady dark eye and the yellow edges on their wing feathers that give the wings a striped effect. Another good mark is the yellow eye-ring, which becomes noticeable on dull birds. In flight, the yellow tail spots are visible.

Most **orange-crowned warblers** are nondescript olive-yellow birds with only a thin broken eye-ring and a faint eyeline. This plainness is, in fact, their best mark.

64

yellow extreme

olive extreme

Orange-crowned Warbler

Yellow Warbler

dull young

♂

♀ and young

WARBLERS

WILSON'S
WARBLER

Yellowthroats are often skulkers except when the male is claiming a territory, openly singing his *wichity, wichity, wichity* song. Also listen for the species' low, husky *chuf* call.

Wilson's warbler and the yellowthroat show yellow and lack wing bars. Both are especially attracted to water. Wilson's is bold and active, picking bugs from foliage and often flycatching. It is likely to be seen in small or medium-sized trees.

The yellowthroat is more secretive but is still often seen in the open. The yellowthroat forages at lower levels in brush and bushes. It behaves a bit like a wren — very active, scolding, and then disappearing in dense brush or briars. Marsh edges and the moister portions of fields are its favorite nesting habitats.

Male **Wilson's warblers** and **common yellowthroats** are distinctively patterned. As with most warblers, it is the females and young birds that present identification problems. The crown of the female Wilson's is always dark, if not as black as the male's. Wilson's also has the distinctive habit of flicking its relatively long tail and holding it cocked expressively.

Best mark for the female yellowthroat is a subtle one. Note how the yellow under the tail and on the breast blends to a brownish gray on the belly. Similar warblers are yellow from breast to tail.

66

Common Yellowthroat

♂

♀

young ♂

Wilson's
Warbler

♀

♂

CHICKADEES AND TITMICE

OAK AND JUNIPER TITMICE

BLACK-CAPPED CHICKADEE

CHESTNUT-BACKED CHICKADEE

MOUNTAIN CHICKADEE

Some of the boldest and also most welcome birds at backyard feeders are the chickadees and the titmice. The birds are closely related and have similar habits. During the summer, they feed mostly on insects and visit feeders infrequently. In winter, they eat seeds and nuts and regularly attend backyard feeders.

Perky crests distinguish the plain gray **titmice.** Coastal birds are a little browner than interior ones and are now considered a separate species. Coastal birds are called oak titmice; interior ones, juniper titmice.

Black-capped chickadees, with their buff sides and black caps and throats, are the most widespread and likely chickadee visitors to most feeders within their range.

Chestnut-backed chickadees are common in residential areas and feeding stations in the Pacific Coast states. In some California birds, the sides can be gray with little or no chestnut.

Mountain chickadees are common at high elevations in summer. Some appear at lowland feeders in winter. **Mountain chickadees** are distinguished by their white eyebrow and gray sides.

Oak and Juniper Titmice

Black-capped Chickadee

Chestnut-backed Chickadee

Mountain Chickadee

BUSHTIT AND KINGLETS

BUSHTIT

RUBY-CROWNED KINGLET

GOLDEN-CROWNED KINGLET

The tiny bushtit and kinglets are the smallest North American songbirds. **Bushtits** are gray-brown and have fairly long tails. Females have pale eyes. Coastal birds have brownish caps, and some interior males in the Southwest have a black patch on the face. When not nesting, bushtits forage in noisy flocks in brush and shrubs from backyards to foothills.

Kinglets are very active birds that nest in coniferous forest and are most often seen in migration and in winter. They visit parks and backyard shrubs and trees but not feeders. The more numerous ruby-crowned kinglet takes a few seeds in winter, but for the most part, kinglets manage to find hidden insect matter even in cold and snowy weather.

The color of their crown and the white eyebrow are good marks for the **golden-crowned kinglet. Ruby-crowned kinglets** are more nondescript; only the male shows red, and it is usually concealed. The tiny bill, plump body, wing-flicking behavior, and short tail distinguish the ruby-crowned from the warblers it might be confused with. The clinching marks are a white eye-ring broken at the top and a white wing bar bordered below by a dark patch — the kinglet patch.

black-eared form

coastal ♂

Bushtit

interior ♂

♀

♂

Ruby-crowned Kinglet

♀

Golden-crowned Kinglet

♀

♂

TOWHEES

SPOTTED TOWHEE

CALIFORNIA TOWHEE

Widely known as the rufous-sided towhee, the spotted towhee was renamed in 1995 by ornithologists who decided it and its very similar eastern relatives (now named eastern towhees) were distinct species.

Brush-loving birds with long rounded tails, towhees are common in backyards, parks, and roadsides, although often hidden. Like the thrashers (p. 44), towhees feed on the ground in the debris and leaf litter under shrubs and bushes. They eat insects as well as seeds.

The rusty-colored sides are good marks for adult **spotted towhees.** Until recently they were called rufous-sided towhees, a much more appropriate and traditional name (see sidebar). Male spotted towhees have black hoods and backs with a variable number of white spots. The black is replaced by gray in adult females. Long black tails with white in the corners are prominent marks in both male and female plumages. Birds just out of the nest are brownish overall and heavily streaked.

The California towhee is especially fond of parks and suburbs. In some suburbs, it is known as the "muffler bird" because of its fondness for hiding under parked cars as if they were brush piles. **California towhees** are dull brown, darker on the tail, paler on the face and throat. There is a hard-to-see patch of rusty color under the tail.

72

Spotted Towhee

California Towhee

GROSBEAKS

Big finches with very heavy bills, the grosbeaks are special visitors to back-yard feeders. Black-headed grosbeaks visit in spring and are often seen in pairs. They eat insects as much as seeds in summer, so they are seldom regular visitors to a sunflower seed station. Evening grosbeaks gather in wandering flocks and often show up at feeders in winter.

Adult male **black-headed grosbeaks** are a striking butterscotch and black that is easy to identify. Also note the white patches in the wings. The female's plumage resembles that of many smaller finches, but her large bill, wash of buff-yellow on the breast, and distinct eyebrow and crown stripes are good marks. There is some fine streaking below, mainly along the sides. Both male and female show yellow in the underwing in flight.

The male **evening grosbeak** is as distinctive as the male black-headed. The large white wing patches, stubby tail, and yellow forehead and eyebrows are all easily seen marks. Females are much grayer and have smaller white wing patches. Evening grosbeaks are attracted by road salt as well as sunflower seeds. They are relatively tame birds that occur irregularly in fall and winter, numerous one year and absent the next.

BLACK-HEADED GROSBEAK

EVENING GROSBEAK

Pine grosbeaks live in the coniferous forest of the Rockies and Pacific Northwest. The male is red with white wing bars; the female, gray with an olive head and rump.

74

Black-headed
Grosbeak

♂

♀

Evening Grosbeak

♂

♀

GOLDFINCHES AND SISKIN

AMERICAN GOLDFINCH

PINE SISKIN

LESSER GOLDFINCH

Lawrence's goldfinch is scarce and irregular in California and Arizona. It shows a lot of yellow in the wings, but not much on the body. Males have a black face.

Some of the most colorful little seed-crunchers are the goldfinches, especially the male American goldfinch in summer. American goldfinches are easily attracted to backyards by thistle seed feeders. Pine siskins and lesser goldfinches also come to backyards and suburbs, although not as commonly.

Female **American goldfinches** and males in fall and winter are a dull, unstreaked olive brown above. The white under their tails and their pale bills are good marks. Males retain their black wings and tail in winter and also a small but bright yellow shoulder patch. Flocks of goldfinches can be recognized by their distinctive roller-coaster flight.

Male **lesser goldfinches** come in two forms, the numerous green-backed and much scarcer black-backed, with some birds intermediate. Females can be safely distinguished from female American goldfinches by the yellow under their tails.

Although they are in the same genus as goldfinches, **pine siskins** show little yellow except in the spread wing. They have a small, sharply pointed bill for a finch — a small mark but a good one separating them from other brown-striped finches.

76

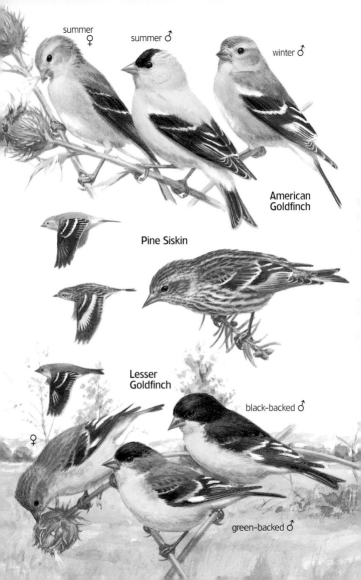

summer ♀

summer ♂

winter ♂

American Goldfinch

Pine Siskin

Lesser Goldfinch

♀

black-backed ♂

green-backed ♂

RED FINCHES

HOUSE FINCH

PURPLE FINCH

Cassin's finch visits feeders in mountain yards. Males are like male purple finches, but the red is brightest on the crown. The nape and back are mostly brown.

The female Cassin's has less pronounced white eyebrows and whisker marks than in the female purple finch. The breast streaks are finer and extend under the tail.

Both the purple and house finches can be seen in backyards. House finches tend to be year-round visitors to a feeder; purple finches visit most often in winter. Calling out a purple finch from among a flock of house finches is a good bird-watching challenge.

Males of both species have a splash of red on them that varies considerably among individuals. Distinguishing one species from another requires care. The females are plain, brown-striped birds that require even more care in identification.

House finches are a little slimmer than **purple finches** and have smaller heads and bills. Side by side the difference is perceptible. Male house finches have brown streaking on their sides and bellies that is lacking in purple finches. The red on the male house finch's head is concentrated on the forehead and eyebrows. On the purple finch, the red extends onto the crown, nape, and back and tends to be more wine-colored.

The contrast of the broad white eyebrow and whisker stripe on the female purple finch is her best mark. The face of the female house finch is much plainer; her breast streaks are a bit finer and extend all the way under her less deeply notched tail.

78

House Finch

Purple Finch

JUNCOS

SLATE-COLORED
JUNCO

GRAY-HEADED
JUNCO

OREGON JUNCO

The white-winged junco inhabits the ponderosa pines of the Black Hills, South Dakota, and has white wing bars. Otherwise it looks much like the slate-colored junco.

N o songbird shows more variation than the junco. Scientists have often reversed themselves on whether the different forms should be classified as species or as races of a single species. Currently all forms are considered races of one species: the dark-eyed junco.

All forms of the **dark-eyed junco** have dark eyes, pale bills, and white outer tail feathers. The white in the tail is especially conspicuous when the bird flies from the ground, where it feeds, to the low branches of a tree.

The slate-colored is the most widespread form of the junco. It is seen during winter and migration in most of the West. Males are slate gray with white bellies. Females are duller, browner, and can show contrast between the hood and the back.

The gray-headed junco of the Rockies and Great Basin has a pale gray head and sides and a rusty-colored back.

The Oregon form is the most numerous in the Pacific Coast states. The male has a black hood, buff to pinkish sides, and a rusty-brown back. Females are duller. In the northern Rockies, Oregon juncos have broader pink sides and a paler hood with a contrasting dark area in front of the eye.

♂ Slate-colored Junco

♀

Gray-headed Junco

♀ Oregon Junco

Oregon Pink-sided Junco

CROWNED SPARROWS

GOLDEN-CROWNED SPARROW

WHITE-CROWNED SPARROW

In both golden- and white-crowned sparrows, the young birds just out of the nest have streaked breasts. The streaks don't last long, perhaps a few weeks at most.

Prominent crown stripes distinguish the golden-crowned and white-crowned sparrows. Both are seen on the ground at feeders in backyards, usually in winter or during migration. The two species often flock and feed together in winter, although golden-crowned sparrows are less numerous than white-crowns and less likely visitors to most backyards.

Both **golden-** and **white-crowned sparrows** are large for sparrows. The golden-crowned is slightly the larger and has duskier underparts. In the white-crowned sparrow, the bill is pink to orange. In the golden-crowned, the upper mandible is dusky; the lower one, pale. These minor points can be useful in identifying some young birds in a mixed flock.

Young birds are not as readily identifiable as the unmistakable adults. Young golden-crowns usually show at least a hint of the adult's crown pattern and color (on the forehead), but it requires imagination to see it at times. Young white-crowned sparrows have brown crown stripes.

Gambel's form of the white-crowned is the most common subspecies in many areas. Its black eyeline stops at the eye instead of continuing in front to the bill. Some coastal birds are browner than those shown.

82

Golden-crowned Sparrow

very young late summer

young

White-crowned Sparrow

Gambel's form

young

very young late summer

DISTINCTIVE SPARROWS

LARK SPARROW

HOUSE SPARROW

Although not common in the West, the tree sparrow can be confused with the lark sparrow. It, too, has a dark breast spot and some rusty or chestnut color on its head. However, it is smaller, slimmer, and has no black head markings or white tail corners.

Lark sparrows tolerate civilization; house sparrows embrace it, abundantly. Winter is the best time to find lark sparrows feeding on the ground in a backyard or local park. Normally birds of open woodlands and grassy areas, they have adapted to roadsides and farmlands. They are very social, living and foraging in small flocks except when nesting.

Lark sparrows have a number of good marks: an elaborate head pattern, white corners in the tail, and a dark spot in the center of a plain breast. The young birds, which are usually seen with adults, have a much less prominent head pattern. Fresh from the nest, the young show a few breast streaks.

House sparrows were introduced to New York from Europe in 1851. After years of expanding their range and numbers, they now blanket the United States and are actually beginning to decline in some areas, although perhaps not at your feeder. Male **house sparrows** have a black bib and chestnut head markings. In fresh plumage (fall), these marks are partially obscured. The female house sparrow is quite plain. Her only good marks are the plain underparts, the pale eyebrow, and the pale bill.

84

very young
late summer

Lark Sparrow

fall ♂

House Sparrow

♀

spring ♂

SPARROWS

CHIPPING
SPARROW

FOX SPARROW

The tree sparrow is closely related to the chipping sparrow, and the two are similar enough to be confused. See the sidebar on page 84.

The chipping sparrow is one of of the smallest sparrows; the fox sparrow, one of the largest. The little chippies are common park and neighborhood birds in summer. They spend more time feeding on lawns, roadsides, and unpaved driveways than they do at feeding stations. In winter, most migrate to the Southwest or out of the United States.

In summer, the **chipping sparrow** has a distinctive rusty crown, a white eyebrow, and a black eyeline that extends through the eye to the bill. Winter birds are harder to identify, but the dark eyeline through the eye together with the gray rump distinguishes it from similar sparrows.

Fox sparrows are regular in residential areas, but they like brush for cover and don't often come out to feed in the open at a feeding station. They are more numerous in brushy canyons and hillsides.

The several western races of the **fox sparrow** show substantial plumage variation, but all have heavy streaking below, which often merges into a central breast spot. The tail is a particularly good mark. Long and blunt (not rounded like the song sparrow's), it is usually rusty red, but some very dark birds have few reddish tones in the tail.

variations

Fox Sparrow

Chipping Sparrow

very young
late summer

first winter

summer

STREAKED SPARROWS

LINCOLN'S SPARROW

SONG SPARROW

SAVANNAH SPARROW

The vesper sparrow can be seen on roadsides or in dry short-grass fields. It has a streaked breast, white eye-ring, and slightly notched tail with white outer feathers.

Brown streaking on the breast is an important mark for many sparrows. Not all birds with streaked breasts are sparrows, however. See the female red-winged blackbird (p. 54), young cowbird (p. 52), finches (p. 78), and pine siskin (p. 76).

Song sparrows are fairly common in backyards, more numerous in brushy parks or streamsides. Lincoln's and savannah sparrows are wary and more reluctant to come out from cover. Lincoln's sparrows like brushy areas in winter. Savannah sparrows are seen in open grassy roadsides, agricultural fields, and parks.

The center breast spot that is often used to identify **song sparrows** is not a conclusive mark; fox sparrows (p. 86) have it, and so do many savannahs and some Lincoln's sparrows. The song sparrow's heavy black whisker mark and long rounded tail should also be noted. **Lincoln's sparrow** is similar to the song sparrow but is smaller, and the breast and the area below the cheek are buff; also note the finer breast streaking and whisker mark.

Savannah sparrows have a short notched tail and usually a fainter whisker mark than the song sparrow has. Many are paler overall than the song sparrow, and some have a yellow spot before the eye.

88

Lincoln's Sparrow

Song Sparrow

young

Savannah
Sparrow

dark

typical

Sooner or later all bird-watchers, even the most casual, wonder how many different species they have seen or how many have visited their backyard. Keeping a record is the only way to know. A list of species seen can become part of the pleasure of bird-watching.

Your backyard list can be put to scientific use by the Cornell Lab of Ornithology. Their Project FeederWatch, begun in 1987 as a joint US-Canadian project with Bird Studies Canada, compiles the counts of backyard birders. Participants receive a research kit and a quarterly newsletter of feeder-watch results for a low annual fee. For more information, call 1-800-843-2473 (1-519-586-3531 in Canada).

✓ Species		Date	Location
○	BREWER'S **B**LACKBIRD 54 *Euphagus cyanocephalus*[1]	....	....
○	RED-WINGED **B**LACKBIRD 54 *Agelaius phoeniceus*	....	....
○	YELLOW-HEADED **B**LACKBIRD 54 *Xanthocephalus xanthocephalus*	....	....
○	MOUNTAIN **B**LUEBIRD 60 *Sialia currucoides*	....	....
○	WESTERN **B**LUEBIRD 60 *Sialia mexicana*	....	....
○	**B**USHTIT 70 *Psaltriparus minimus*	....	....
○	**C**ATBIRD 60 Gray Catbird[2] *Dumetella carolinensis*	....	....

[1] Names in *italics* are the scientific names adopted by the American Ornithologists' Union.
[2] When the AOU English name differs from the common name as used in this guide, the official AOU English name is given on the second line.

☑ Species	Date	Location
○ BLACK-CAPPED CHICKADEE 68 *Parus atricapillus*		
○ CHESTNUT-BACKED CHICKADEE 68 *Parus rufescens*		
○ CALIFORNIA CONDOR 20 *Gymnogyps californianus*		
○ BROWN-HEADED COWBIRD 52 *Molothrus ater*		
○ BROWN CREEPER 38 *Certhia americana*		
○ AMERICAN CROW 48 *Corvus brachyrhynchos*		
○ MOURNING DOVE 32 *Zenaida macroura*		
○ ROCK DOVE 32 *Columba livia*		
○ HOUSE FINCH 78 *Carpodacus mexicanus*		
○ PURPLE FINCH 78 *Carpodacus purpureus*		
○ RED-SHAFTED FLICKER 36 Northern Flicker *Colaptes auratus*		
○ ASH-THROATED FLYCATCHER 40 *Myiarchus cinerascens*		
○ AMERICAN GOLDFINCH 76 *Carduelis tristis*		
○ LESSER GOLDFINCH 76 *Carduelis psaltria*		
○ BLACK-HEADED GROSBEAK 74 *Pheucticus melanocephalus*		
○ EVENING GROSBEAK 74 *Coccothraustes vespertinus*		
○ COOPER'S HAWK 24 *Accipiter cooperii*		

✓ Species	Date	Location

		Date	Location
○ RED-TAILED **H**AWK 22 *Buteo jamaicensis*		....	....
○ SHARP-SHINNED **H**AWK 24 *Accipiter striatus*		....	....
○ ANNA'S **H**UMMINGBIRD 28 *Calypte anna*		....	....
○ BLACK-CHINNED **H**UMMINGBIRD 28 *Archilochus alexandri*		....	....
○ BROAD-TAILED **H**UMMINGBIRD 28 *Selasphorus platycercus*		....	....
○ RUFOUS **H**UMMINGBIRD 28 *Selasphorus rufus*		....	....
○ PINYON **J**AY 50 *Gymnorhinus cyanocephalus*		....	....
WESTERN SCRUB-JAY *see* **S**CRUB-JAY			
○ STELLER'S **J**AY 50 *Cyanocitta stelleri*		....	....
○ DARK-EYED **J**UNCO 80 *Junco hyemalis*		....	....
○ **K**ESTREL 22 American Kestrel *Falco sparverius*		....	....
○ EASTERN **K**INGBIRD 40 *Tyrannus tyrannus*		....	....
○ WESTERN **K**INGBIRD 40 *Tyrannus verticalis*		....	....
○ GOLDEN-CROWNED **K**INGLET 70 *Regulus satrapa*		....	....
○ RUBY-CROWNED **K**INGLET 70 *Regulus calendula*		....	....
○ BLACK-BILLED **M**AGPIE 46 *Pica pica*		....	....
○ WESTERN **M**EADOWLARK 56 *Sturnella neglecta*		....	....

✓ Species		Date	Location

MOCKINGBIRD   46
Northern Mockingbird
Mimus polyglottos

COMMON **N**IGHTHAWK   18
Chordeiles minor

RED-BREASTED **N**UTHATCH 38
Sitta canadensis

WHITE-BREASTED **N**UTHATCH 38
Sitta carolinensis

BULLOCK'S **O**RIOLE   56
Icterus bullockii

BARN **O**WL   18
Tyto alba

GREAT HORNED **O**WL   18
Bubo virginianus

RING-NECKED **P**HEASANT 30
Phasianus colchicus

BLACK **P**HOEBE   42
Sayornis nigricans

SAY'S **P**HOEBE   42
Sayornis saya

PIGEON
see ROCK **D**OVE

BAND-TAILED **P**IGEON   32
Columba fasciata

CALIFORNIA **Q**UAIL   30
Callipepla californica

GAMBEL'S **Q**UAIL   30
Callipepla gambelii

COMMON **R**AVEN   48
Corvus corax

ROBIN   58
American robin
Turdus migratorius

WESTERN **S**CRUB-JAY   50
Aphelocoma californica

✓ Species		Date	Location
○ PINE **S**ISKIN *Carduelis pinus*	76	....	....
○ CHIPPING **S**PARROW *Spizella passerina*	86	....	....
○ FOX **S**PARROW *Passerella iliaca*	86	....	....
○ GOLDEN-CROWNED **S**PARROW *Zonotrichia atricapilla*	82	....	....
○ HOUSE **S**PARROW *Passer domesticus*	84	....	....
○ LARK **S**PARROW *Chondestes grammacus*	84	....	....
○ LINCOLN'S **S**PARROW *Melospiza lincolnii*	88	....	....
○ SAVANNAH **S**PARROW *Passerculus sandwichensis*	88	....	....
○ SONG **S**PARROW *Melospiza melodia*	88	....	....
○ WHITE-CROWNED **S**PARROW *Zonotrichia leucophrys*	82	....	....
○ **S**TARLING European Starling *Sturnus vulgaris*	52	....	....
○ BARN **S**WALLOW *Hirundo rustica*	26	....	....
○ CLIFF **S**WALLOW *Hirundo pyrrhonota*	26	....	....
○ TREE **S**WALLOW *Tachycineta bicolor*	26	....	....
○ WESTERN **T**ANAGER *Piranga ludoviciana*	58	....	....
○ CALIFORNIA **T**HRASHER *Toxostoma redivivum*	44	....	....
○ JUNIPER **T**ITMOUSE *Baeolophus ridgwayi*	68	....	....

✓ Species		Date	Location
○ OAK **T**ITMOUSE *Baeolophus inornatus*	68	....	....
○ CALIFORNIA **T**OWHEE *Pipilo crissalis*	72	....	....
○ SPOTTED **T**OWHEE *Pipilo maculatus*	72	....	....
○ TURKEY **V**ULTURE *Cathartes aura*	20	....	....
○ AUDUBON'S **W**ARBLER Yellow-rumped Warbler *Dendroica coronata*	62	....	....
○ ORANGE-CROWNED **W**ARBLER *Vermivora celata*	64	....	....
○ TOWNSEND'S **W**ARBLER *Dendroica townsendi*	62	....	....
○ WILSON'S **W**ARBLER *Wilsonia pusilla*	66	....	....
○ YELLOW **W**ARBLER *Dendroica petechia*	64	....	....
○ CEDAR **W**AXWING *Bombycilla cedrorum*	42	....	....
○ ACORN **W**OODPECKER *Melanerpes formicivorus*	36	....	....
○ DOWNY **W**OODPECKER *Picoides pubescens*	34	....	....
○ HAIRY **W**OODPECKER *Picoides villosus*	34	....	....
○ LADDER-BACKED **W**OODPECKER *Picoides scalaris*	36	....	....
○ BEWICK'S **W**REN *Thryomanes bewickii*	44	....	....
○ HOUSE **W**REN *Troglodytes aedon*	44	....	....
○ COMMON **Y**ELLOWTHROAT *Geothlypsis trichas*	66	....	....

Want to Help Conserve Birds?

It's As Easy As ABC!

By becoming a member of the American
Bird Conservancy, you can help ensure
work is being done to protect many of the
species in this field guide. You can receive *Bird
Conservation* magazine quarterly to learn about bird
conservation throughout the Americas and *World Birdwatch*
magazine for information on international bird conservation.

Make a difference to birds.
Copy this card and mail to the address listed below.

☐ **Yes,** I want to become a member and receive *Bird
       Conservation* magazine.
       A check in the amount of $15 is enclosed.

☐ **Yes,** I want to become an international member of
       ABC and receive both *Bird Conservation* and
       World Birdwatch magazines.
       A check in the amount of $40 is enclosed.

NAME

ADDRESS

CITY/STATE/ZIP CODE

Return to: American Bird Conservancy
1250 24th Street NW, Suite 400, Washington, D.C. 20037
or call **1-888-BIRD-MAG** or e-mail: abc@abcbirds.org

Memberships are tax deductible to the extent allowable by law.